200 QUOTES THAT WILL CHANGE THE WAY YOU THINK

BOOKGAINS

"THIS IS THE BOOK I ALWAYS WANTED TO HAVE. I KNOW THAT THERE ARE A BUNCH OF QUOTE BOOKS AVAILABLE IN THE MARKET BUT THIS IS SPECIAL BECAUSE THIS BOOK IS A COMPILATION OF QUOTES THAT ARE MY FAVORITES, QUOTES THAT I WILL READ FROM THIS BOOK EVERYDAY TO THINK BETTER, DO BETTER AND LIVE BETTER. I HOPE YOU WILL DO THE SAME"

—MOHIT PANCHAL

"We learn not in the school, but in life."

— SENECA

"Life is long if you know how to use it."

— SENECA

"Everyone thinks of changing the world, but no one thinks of changing himself."

— LEO TOLSTOY

"The secret of health for both mind and body is...live the present moment wisely and earnestly."

— BUDDHA

"The goal of life is living in agreement with nature"

— ZENO OF CITIUM

"Remember that even if you were to live for three thousand years, or thirty thousand, you could not lose any other life than the one you have, and there will be no other life after it. So the longest and the shortest lives are the same. The present moment is shared by all living creatures, but the time that is past is gone forever. No one can lose the past or the future, for if they don't belong to you, how can they be taken from you?"

— MARCUS AURELIUS

"Those who cannot change their minds cannot change anything."

— GEORGE BERNARD SHAW

"The two most important days in life are the day you born and the day you find out why."

— MARK TWAIN

"He who has a why to live can bear almost any how."

— FRIEDRICH NIETZSCHE

"Great minds have purposes, others have wishes."

— WASHINGTON IRVIN

"Desire is a contract that you make with yourself to be unhappy until you get what you want."

— NAVAL RAVIKANT

"Do not spoil what you have by desiring what you have not; remember that what you now have was once among the things you only hoped for."

— EPICURUS

"Have a burning desire to make this world more beautiful for those who live here and for those who are yet to come. If desire resolves around pleasures, avoid them."

— **MOHIT PANCHAL**

"A Stoic is someone who transforms fear into prudence, pain into transformation, mistakes into initiation, and desires into undertaking."

— NASSIM NICHOLAS TALEB

"I take pleasure in my transformations. I look quiet and consistent, but few know how many women there are in me."

— ANAIS NIN

"Success comes from the inside out. In order to change what is on the outside, you must first change what is on the inside."

— IDOWU KOYENIKAN

"As you start to walk on the way, the way appears."

— RUMI

"There is no other greater ecstasy, than to know who you are."

— OSHO

"Expansion is Life, Contraction is Death."

— SWAMI VIVEKANANDA

"The struggles we endure today will be the 'good old days' we laugh about tomorrow."

— AARON LAURITSEN

"Today is yours to shape.

Create a masterpiece!"
— STEVE MARABOLI

"Focus your mind on a few important tasks of your day and when you will achieve them, your confidence will automatically increase."

— MOHIT PANCHAL

"We are living in a culture entirely hypnotized by the illusion of time, in which the so-called present moment is felt as nothing but an infinitesimal hairline between an all-powerfully causative past and an absorbingly important future.

— ALAN WATTS

"The Mind must be given relaxation. It will rise improved and sharper after a good break."

— SENECA

"Freedom isn't secured by filling up on your heart's desire but by removing your desire."

— EPICTETUS

"Better to fail in Imagination than to succeed in limitation."

— HERMAN MELVILLE

"As soon as you trust yourself, you will know how to live."

— VAN GOETHE

"Choose not to be harmed—and you won't feel harmed. Don't feel harmed—and you haven't been."

— MARCUS AURELIUS

"We can ignore reality, but we cannot ignore the consequences of ignoring reality."

— AYN RAND

"Do not be satisfied with the stories that come before you. Unfold your own myth"

— RUMI

"After 45 years of research and study, the best advice I can give to people is to be a little kinder to each other."

— ALDOUS HUXLEY

"The trouble is, you think you have time."

— BUDDHA

"It's not what we do once in a while that shapes our lives, but what we do consistently."

— TONY ROBBINS

"Life is a tragedy for those who feel, and a comedy for those who think."

— JEAN DE LA BRUYERE

"Life isn't about finding yourself. Life is about creating yourself."

— GEORGE BERNARD SHAW

"All truths that kept silent become poisonous."

— FRIEDRICH NIETZSCHE

"An intellectual is someone whose mind watches itself."

— ALBERT CAMUS

"The most important decision you make is to be in a good mood."

— VOLTAIRE

"To be a philosopher is to solve some of the problems of life, not only theoretically, but practically."

— HENRY DAVID THOREAU

"One day in retrospect, the years of struggle will strike you as the most beautiful."

— SIGMUND FREUD

"Your real resume is just a catalog of all your suffering. If I ask you to describe our real life to yourself, and you look back from your deathbed at the interesting things you've done, it's all going to be around the sacrifices you made, the hard things you did."

— **NAVAL RAVIKANT**

"A man is great not because he hasn't failed; a man is great because failure hasn't stopped him."

— CONFUCIUS

"Be a loner. That gives you time to wonder, to search for the truth. Have holy curiosity. Make your life worth living."

— **ALBERT EINSTEIN**

"Enlightenment is man's leaving his selfcaused immaturity."

— IMMANUEL KANT

"A man's maturity consists in having found again the seriousness one had as a child, at play."

— FRIEDRICH NIETZSCHE

"Wealth is the slave of a wise man and the master of a fool."

— SENECA

"I am a slow walker, but I never walk back."

— ABRAHAM LINCOLN

"He who laughs at himself never runs out of things to laugh at."

— SENECA

"The secret of happiness is not found in seeking more, but in developing the capacity to enjoy less."

— BUDDHA

"You talk when you cease to be at peace with your thoughts."

— KAHLIL GIBRAN

"Drop the idea of becoming someone, because you are already a masterpiece. You cannot be improved. You have only to come to it, to know it, to realize it."

—OSHO

"Only two things can reveal life's great secrets: suffering and love."

— PAULO COELHO

"A life of short duration...could be so rich in joy and love that it could contain more meaning than a life lasting eighty years."

— VICTOR FRANKL

"The purpose of life is to bring forth goodness. Now, in this life."

— LEO TOLSTOY

"A dreamer is one who can only find his way by moonlight, and his punishment is that he can see the dawn before the rest of the world."

— OSCAR WILDE

"History shows that the less people read, the more books they buy."

— ALBERT CAMUS

"An intellectual says a simple thing in a hard way. An artist says a hard thing in a simple way."

— CHARLES BUKOWSKI

"We learn about life not from pluses alone, but from minuses as well."

— ANTON CHEKOV

"By failing to prepare, you are preparing to fail."

— BENJAMIN FRANKLIN

"Iron rusts from disuse; water loses its purity from stagnation, even so does inaction sap the vigor of the mind."

— LEONARDO DA VINCI

"Talking without thinking is shooting without thinking."

— MIGUEL DE CARVANTES

"How many things would you attempt, if you knew you could not fail?"

— ROBERT FROST

"It is a shame for a man to grow old without seeing the beauty and strength of which his body is capable."

— SOCRATES

"Don't judge each day by the harvest you reap but by the seeds that you plant."

— ROBERT LOUIS STEVENSON

"Wealth is like seawater: the more we drink, the thirstier we become. And the same is true for fame."

— ARTHUR SCHOPENHAUER

"Half the world is composed of people who have something to say but can't, and the other half who have nothing to say and keep on saying it."

— ROBERT FROST

"There are thousand lessons in defeat but only one in victory."

— CONFUCIUS

"Never argue with a fool, onlookers may not be able to tell the difference."

— MARK TWAIN

"Knowledge isn't power until it's applied."

— DALE CARNEGIE

"The only real mistake is the one from which we learn nothing."

— HENRY FORD

"Care about what other people think and you will always be their prisoner."

— LAO TZU

74

"Knowledge speaks, but wisdom listens."

— JIMI HENDRIX

"Don't hope that events will turn out the way you want, welcome events in whichever way they happen: this is the path to peace."

— EPICTETUS

"A man sees in the world what he carries in the heart."

— GOETHE

"A ship in harbour is safe, but that is not what ships are built for."

— JOHN A. SHEDD

"Sadness gives depth. Happiness gives height. Sadness gives roots. Happiness gives branches."

— OSHO

"Growth is painful. Change is painful. But nothing is as painful as staying stuck somewhere you don't belong."
— MANDY HALE

"The meaning of life is not to be discovered only after death in some hidden, mysterious realm. On the contrary, it can be found by eating the succulent fruit of the Tree of Life and by living in the here and now as fully and creatively as we can."

— PAUL KURTZ

"The purpose of life is not to be happy. It is to be useful, to be honourable, to be compassionate, to have it make some difference that you have lived and lived well."

— RALPH WALDO EMERSON

"We are what we repeatedly do. Excellence, then, is not an act but a habit."

— ARISTOTLE

"The greatest enemy of knowledge is not ignorance, it is the illusion of knowledge."

— STEPHEN HAWKING

"The two most important days in your life are the day you are born and the day you find out why."

— MARK TWAIN

"Do not dwell in the past, do not dream of the future, concentrate the mind on the present moment."

— BUDDHA

"In the midst of movement and chaos, keep stillness inside of you."

— DEEPAK CHOPRA

"The quality of your life is in direct proportion to the amount of uncertainty you can comfortably deal with."

— TONY ROBBINS

"Don't let the others' opinions drown out your own inner voice."

— STEVE JOBS

"The only thing standing between you and your goal is the story you keep telling yourself as to why you can't achieve it."

— JORDAN BELFORT

"The future is always beginning now."

— MARK STRAND

"It is our choices, Harry, that show what we truly are, far more than our abilities."

— **ALBUS DUMBLEDORE**

(*harry potter series*)

"I have learned to seek my happiness by limiting my desires rather than attempting to satisfy them."

— SENECA THE YOUNGER

"If you make the easy choices right now, your overall life will be a lot harder."

— NAVAL RAVIKANT

"Try not to become a man of success, but rather try to become a man of value."

— ALBERT EINSTEIN

"The only way to do great work is to love what you do."

— STEVE JOBS

"Stop living same year 75 times and call it life."

—ROBIN SHARMA

"The two most powerful warriors are patience and time."

— LEO TOLSTOY

"Life is long enough
if you know how to
use it."

— SENECA

"The mind is everything. What you think, you become."

— BUDDHA

"A fit body, a calm mind, a house full of love. These things cannot be bought – they must be earned."

— NAVAL RAVIKANT

"Life is like riding a bicycle. To keep your balance, you must keep moving."

— ALBERT EINSTEIN

"If the WHY is powerful,

the HOW is easy."

— JIM ROHN

"Those who keep learning will keep rising in life."

— CHARLIE MUNGER

"Read to expand your mind.

Write to organize your mind.

Build to focus your mind."

— DAN KOE

"The universe has some great things in store for you after you go through this hard part."

— PHIL GOOD

"The man who graduates today and stops learning tomorrow is uneducated the day after."

— NEWTON D. BAKER

"If we don't discipline ourselves the world will do it for us."

—WILLIAM FEATHER

"Those who think they have no time for bodily exercise will sooner or later have to find time for illness."

— EDWARD STANLEY

"You are the only person who can give yourself what you want."

— LEWIS HOWES

"Always do what you are afriad to do."

— RALPH WALDO EMERSON

"You can make more friends in two months by becoming interested in other people than you can in two years bytrying to get other people interested in you."

— DALE CARNEGIE

"Read more books. Walk in nature daily. Let go of the past. Drink more water. Say thank you a lot. Get up at 5 am. Smile at strangers. Keep a journal."

— ROBIN SHARMA

"If you can't change your fate, change your attitude."

— AMY TAN

"Clear thinking and good judgement is a cheat code to life."

— NAVAL RAVIKANT

"Accept both compliments and critisism. Because a flower to grow takes both sun and rain."

— AN OLD SAYING

"Half of the troubles of this life can be traced to saying yes too quickly and not saying no soon enough."

— JOSH BILLINGS

"Happiness cannot be pursued; it must ensue."

— VICTOR FRANKL

"Life is really simple, but we insist on making it complicated."

— CONFUCIUS

"When we strive to become than we are, everything around us become better too."

— PAULO COELHO

"Being deeply loved by someone gives you strength, while loving someone deeply gives you courage."

— LAO TZU

"The training is nothing.
The will is everything.
The will to act."

— BATMAN BEGINS

"There is no past and no future; no one has ever entered those two imaginary kingdoms. There is only the present."

— LEO TOLSTOY

"Life's battles don't always go to the stronger or faster man, But soon or late the man who wins is the man who thinks he can!"

— NAPOLEAN HILL

124

"Difficulties strengthen the mind, as labor does the body."

— SENECA

"Difficulty is what wakes up the genius."

— NASSIM NICHOLAS TALEB

"True love is born from understanding."

— BUDDHA

"Thinking is difficult, that is why most people judge."

— CARL JUNG

"Think of yourself as dead. You have lived your life. Now take what's left and live it properly."

— MARCUS AURELIUS

"If you can gain control over 60 percent of the time in your life, you are really successful."

— ROD STEIGER

"It's hard to beat a person who never gives up."

— BABE RUTH

"There are two medicines for all ills: Time and Silence."

— ALEXANDRE DUMAS

"Men's natures are alike,
it is their habits that
carry them far apart."

— CONFUCIUS

"Your time is limited, so don't waste it living someone else's life."

— STEVE JOBS

"You practice and you get better. It's very simple."

— PHILIP GLASS

"Do what you can, with what you have, where you are."

— THEODORE ROOSEVELT

"Go to the edge of the cliff andjump off. Build your wings on the way down."

— RAY BRADBURY

"Do not conceive that fine clothes make fine men, any more than fine feathers make fine birds."

— GEORGE WASHINGTON

"95% people are reacting to life, they are not living at all."

— BOB PROCTOR

"Reading is essential for those who seek to rise above the ordinary."

— JIM ROHN

"Life is like riding a bicycle. To keep your balance, you must keep moving."

— ALBERT EINSTEIN

"Don't let where you are become a ceiling on where you can go."

— SHANE PARRISH

"The more that you read, the more things you will know. The more that you learn, the more places you will go."

— DR. SEUSS

"The most important days in your life are the day you are born and the day you find out why."

— MARK TWAIN

"There are two vices much darker and more serious than the rest: lack of persistence and lack of self control."

— MARCUS AURELIUS

"Compare yourself to who you were yesterday, not to who someone else is today."

— JORDAN PETERSON

"Problems always appear big when incompetent men are working on them."

— WILLIAM FEATHER

"Life is a balance between holding on and letting go."

— RUMI

"Be where you are; otherwise you will miss your life."

— BUDDHA

"If we encounter a man of rare intellect, we should ask him what books he reads."

— RALPH WALDO EMERSON

150

"You easily waste years when you keep thinking you still have time."

"It does not matter what you bear, but how you bear it."

— SENECA

"The cold water does not get warmer if you jump late."

— UNKNOWN

"Fear defeat more people than any other one thing in the world."

— RALPH WALDO EMERSON

"Life is not about finding yourself. Life is about creating yourself."

— GEORGE BERNARD SHAW

"You do not write your life with words... You write it with actions. What you think is not important. It is only important what you do."

— PATRICK NESS

"Keep this thought at the ready at daybreak, and through the day and night—there is only one path to happiness, and that is in giving up all outside of your sphere of choice, re garding nothing else as your possession, surrendering all else to God and Fortune."

— EPICTETUS

"Beautiful days do not come to you. You must walk towards them."

— RUMI

"Keep away from people who try to belittle your ambitions, small people always do that, but the really great make you feel that you, too, can become great."

— MARK TWAIN

"The world breaks everyone and afterward many are strong at the broken places."

— ERNEST HEMINGWAY

"The poorest man I know is the man who has nothing but money."

— UNKNOWN

"He who flatters a man is his enemy, he who tells him of his faults is his maker."

— CONFUCIUS

"When you're finished changing, you're finished."

— BENJAMIN FRANKLIN

"I keep six honest serving men [they taught me all I knew]. Their Names are What and Why and When and How and Where and Who."

— RUDYARD KIPLING

"To see what is right and not do it is the worst cowardice."

— CONFUCIUS

"In Anger, we should refrain both from speech and action."

— PYTHAGORAS

"When true virtue is lost, Good Nature appears. When good Nature is lost, Justice appears. When Justice is lost, Decency appears. The rules of Decency are only a semblance of Truth and the beginning of all Disorder."

— LAO TZU

"It is easier to prevent bad habits than to break them."

— BENJAMIN FRANKLIN

"Friendship is one mind in two bodies."

— MENCIUS

"The whole secret of a successful life is to find out what is one's destiny to do, and then do it."

— HENRY FORD

"Do not pray for an easy life, pray for the strength to endure a difficult one."

— BUCE LEE

"Be who you are and say what you feel because those who mind don't matter and those who matter don't mind."

— DR. SEUSS

"Courage is knowing what not to fear."

— PLATO

"In the end, it's not the years in your life that count. It's the life in your years."

— ABRAHAM LINCOLN

174

"Whoever is happy will make others happy too."

— ANNE FRANK

"A tiger doesn't lose sleep over the opinion of sheep."

— UNKNOWN

"Live each day as if your life had just begun."

— GOETHE

"Love yourself first and everything else falls into line. You really have to yourself to get anything done in this world."

— LUCILLE BALL

"If you look at what you have in life, you'll always have more."

— OPRAH WINFREY

"If I cannot do great things, I can do small things in a great way."

— MARTIN LUTHER KING JR.

"You don't always need a plan. Sometimes you just need to breathe, trust, let go, and see what happens."

— MANDY TALE

"Some people look for a beautiful place. Others make a place beautiful."

— HAZRAT INAYAT KHAN

"If you can dream it, you can achieve it."

— ZIG ZIGLAR

"The bad news is time flies. The good news is you're the pilot."

— MICHAEL ALTSHULER

"Before you speak, let your words pass through three gates: Is it true? Is it necessary? Is it kind?"

— BUDDHA

"Real life is about reacting quickly to the opportunity at hand, not the opportunity you envisioned. Not thinking and scheming for the future, but letting it happen."

— CONAN O'BRIEN

"The measure of intelligence is the ability to change."

— ALBERT EINSTEIN

"You've got to listen to the voice in your gut. It is individual. It is unique. It is yours. It's called being authentic."

— MEREDITH VIEIRA

"When adversity hits, go out and learn something."

— JULIE ANDREWS

"You can't put a limit on anything. The more you dream, the farther you get."

— MICHAEL PHELPS

"When you have a great and difficult task, something perhaps almost impossible, if you only work a little at a time, every day little, suddenly the work will finish itself."

— ISAK DINESEN

"The way to get started is to quit talking and begin doing."

— WALT DISNEY

"A man is a success if he gets up in the morning and gets to bed at night, and in between he does what he wants to do."

— BOB DYLAN

"If you don't have confidence, you'll always find a way not to win."

— CARL LEWIS

"Do what you can, with what you have, where you are."

— THEODORE ROOSEVELT

"Expose yourself to your deepest fear; after that, fear has no power, and the fear of freedom shrinks and vanishes. You are free."

— JIM MORRISON

"Character consists of what you do on the third and fourth tries."

— JAMES A. MICHENER

"Get into your life and do what you enjoy and be the best at what you can be. Maybe you won't be successful and rich by the world's standards, but you will have the best life capable of having. If you don't do that, you're cheating yourself."

— ARTIE SHAW

"Don't worry about things. Don't push. Just do your work and you'll survive. The important thing is to have a ball, to be joyful, to be loving, and to be explosive. Out of that comes everything and you grow."

— RAY BRADBURY

"Respect life, revere life. There is nothing more holy than life, nothing more divine than life."

— OSHO

"Stay Hungry, Stay Foolish."

— STEVE JOBS

Thank you to each and everyone who gave their time to read this book. You guys are amazing and I must inform you that we have a beautiful community of book readers across different platforms and I would be happy to see you there joining other readers 😊

Instagram.com/itsbookgains

Youtube.com/@bookgains

Threads.net/itsbookgains

Twitter.com/itsbookgains